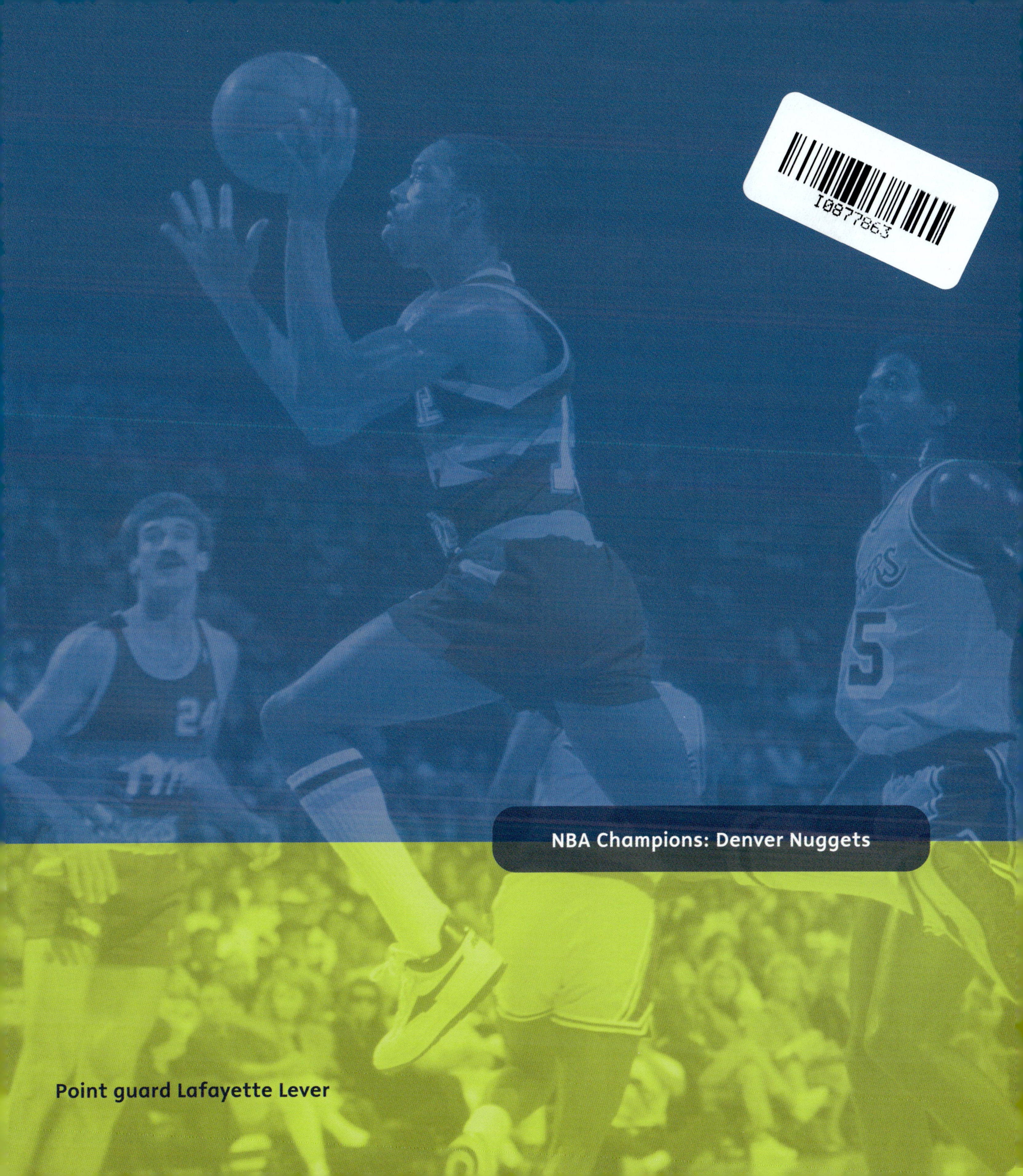

NBA Champions: Denver Nuggets

Point guard Lafayette Lever

Power forward Kenyon Martin

NBA CHAMPIONS

DENVER NUGGETS

JOE TISCHLER

CREATIVE EDUCATION / CREATIVE PAPERBACKS

Forward David Thompson

Published by Creative Education and Creative Paperbacks
P.O. Box 227, Mankato, Minnesota 56002
Creative Education and Creative Paperbacks are imprints of
The Creative Company
www.thecreativecompany.us

Art Direction by Tom Morgan
Book production by Graham Morgan
Edited by Grace Cain

Images by Getty Images/AAron Ontiveroz, cover, Andrew D. Bernstein, 5, 15-16, Brian Babineau, 2, Carl Iwasaki, 4, Dick Raphael, 6, Doug Pensinger, 24, Garrett Ellwood, 3, Harry How, 20, Heinz Kluetmeier, 12, Icon Sportswire, 10, Mike Powell, 1, Richard Mackson, cover, Tim DeFrisco, 19, Unknown, 9, Wally Skalij, 7

Library of Congress Cataloging-in-Publication Data
Names: Tischler, Joe, author.
Title: Denver Nuggets / by Joe Tischler.
Other titles: Creative sports: NBA champions.
Description: Mankato, Minnesota : Creative Education and Creative Paperbacks, [2025] | Series: Creative sports: NBA champions | Includes index. | Audience: Ages 7-10 | Audience: Grades 2-3 | Summary: "Elementary-level text and dynamic sports photos highlight the NBA championship win of the Denver Nuggets, plus sensational players associated with the professional basketball team such as Nikola Jokić"— Provided by publisher.
Identifiers: LCCN 2024014040 (print) | LCCN 2024014041 (ebook) | ISBN 9798889892540 (library binding) | ISBN 9781682776209 (paperback) | ISBN 9798889893653 (ebook)
Subjects: LCSH: Denver Nuggets (Basketball team)—History—Juvenile literature. | CYAC: Denver Nuggets (Basketball team)—History.
Classification: LCC GV885.52.D46 T57 2025 (print) | LCC GV885.52.D46 (ebook) | DDC 796.323/640978883—dc23/eng/20240402
LC record available at https://lccn.loc.gov/2024014040
LC ebook record available at https://lccn.loc.gov/2024014041

Printed in China

Shooting guard Elston Turner

Forward Kiki Vandeweghe

CONTENTS

Home of the Nuggets

Denver, Colorado, is a city near the Rocky Mountains. The city's nickname is the "Mile High City." The town sits one mile above sea level. Denver is also home to an **arena** called Ball Arena. It's home to a basketball team called the Nuggets.

The Denver Nuggets are a National Basketball Association (NBA) team. They play in the Northwest Division. That's part of the Western Conference. Their **rivals** are the Utah Jazz and Minnesota Timberwolves. All NBA teams want to win the NBA Finals and become champions.

Forward Michael Porter Jr.

Naming the Nuggets

The team was first called the Rockets. They changed their name to the Nuggets in 1974. People rushed to the Rocky Mountains in Colorado in the 1800s. They were searching for gold and silver nuggets. The team is named the Nuggets to honor this history. Denver had an NBA team in 1949–50. They were also called the Nuggets.

Guard David Thompson

Nuggets History

The Nuggets began play in 1967. They played in the American Basketball Association (ABA). Center Spencer Haywood was great in 1970. He won both the ABA **Most Valuable Player (MVP)** and Rookie of the Year awards.

The team moved to the NBA in 1976. High-flying guard David Thompson and steady center Dan Issel were key stars. Denver reached the conference finals in their second season as part of the NBA. Alex English and Lafayette "Fat" Lever kept Denver winning throughout the 1980s. They made the playoffs nine straight seasons.

Many losing seasons followed. Denver won just 11 games in 1997–98. Super-scorer Carmelo Anthony came in 2003. He led Denver to their first playoff appearance in nine years. The Nuggets reached the conference finals in 2009.

Forward Carmelo Anthony

Point guard Chauncey Billups

Center Nikola Jokić joined the team in 2015. He became one of the best players in the league. He was named NBA MVP in 2021, 2022, and 2024. In 2023, he led the Nuggets to their first NBA Finals appearance. Denver beat the Miami Heat in five games. The Nuggets were champions for the first time!

Other Nuggets Stars

The Nuggets have had many other great stars. Forward Bobby Jones was a great defender in the 1970s. He was an **all-star** five times. Dikembe Mutombo was great at defense, too. Three times he led the league in blocked shots. He won the Defensive Player of the Year Award in 1995.

Center Dikembe Mutombo

Center Nikola Jokić

Andre Miller and Chauncey Billups were great point guards. They dished out a lot of **assists**. Ty Lawson was also good at giving assists.

Today, Jamal Murray teams with Jokić to form one of the game's best duos. Michael Porter Jr. and Aaron Gordon are quality starters. Nuggets' fans hope they can help bring another **title** to Denver soon!

About the Nuggets

First season: 1967–68

Conference/division: Western Conference, Northwest Division

Team colors: navy blue, red, and yellow

Home arena: Ball Arena

NBA CHAMPIONSHIPS:

2023, 4 games to 1 over Miami Heat

TEAM WEBSITE:

https://www.nba.com/nuggets/

Glossary

all-star—a player picked to play in the All-Star Game, featuring the season's top stars

arena—a large building with seats for spectators, where sports games and entertainment events are held

assist—a basketball pass that leads to a basket

Most Valuable Player (MVP)—an honor given to the season's best player

rival—a team that plays extra hard against another team

title—another word for championship

Center/power forward Chris Andersen

Index